Illegal but legal

The misadventures of nation-state actors

CAUTION

This book does not reveal any dangerous information.

This book just describes Nation-state actors and their work.

We are not responsible for whatever you do by reading this book.

Do not try to hack others property, it is harmfull to victim and you as well.

Imagine James bond. bond goes on a mission he gets some vital equipment from q on one mission, he got a special ring, had a way to emit an ultra-high-frequency which when put up to a window shattered the glass, on this mission bond snuck into North Korea undetected but imagine what kind of consequences in which he would be if he lost the ring while in North Korea? and if the North Korean government found the ring? it would analyze it and they would discover its cutting-edge technology and possibly be able to reproduce that technology for themselves essentially putting the technology in the wrong hands when analyzing the ring they may even be able

to track down as origins to mi5 this would mean that just by finding the ring alone north Korea could deduct that, there was a British spy in their country

this could cause numerous problems maybe even a war in the internet world where governments hack other governments. It's crucial to not let the enemy know you're there or capture you're hacking techniques because if they do it could have devastating consequences

This Book written by Shaheer Ahmed has a true story from the dark side of the Internet I'm Shaheer, this book may seem like child's play to me I'm even nervous to tell it I don't think I'm in the FBI

watch list now but I probably will be after this book. let me ask you this who is the most sophisticated hacking

team in the world? it's a team comprised of graduates from MIT and Carnegie Mellon a team that has created the most cutting-edge hacking tools, a team that can utilize an almost unlimited amount of resources like language interpreters huge data centers and supercomputers, a team that has a history of creating encryption methods and building the Internet. Yes, the hacking groups that are inside government agencies otherwise known as the nation-state actors and most of what they do is considered top-secret so getting one of them to speak for this book is a very special privilege. nation-state actors are an exceptional group of hackers because they essentially have license to hack. They work without the fear of legal retribution they are often tasked with stealing secrets or disrupting the target through connected networks and it's important that all of what they do goes entirely under the radar and is invisible to the target don't ask me how I found this and don't ask me who but in this book we will hear a story from a person who has been in the innermost bowels of one of the most elite hacking teams in the world yeah I spent almost 1 year

running offensive cyber operations so I have many many
stories the only way they would agree to be interviewed for this book was if I
kept them anonymous and disguised. You might wonder whether their story is true or not but you need to agree with it,
pretty much all governments have an intelligence department, the US has the Central Intelligence Agency in the National Security Agency and others the goal of the intelligence department is to get information on enemies regarding threats to the nation this is done in
the name of national security in short governments spy on each other this shouldn't be news to you it's been happening for centuries in the past
spies would go undercover and physically break into places to extract secret data they were highly trained at being stealthy being able to escape and evade
are often excellent drivers but now government's rely on computers to communicate store data and create plans this exposes a whole new attack surface instead of physically breaking into a building to steal documents hackers can

steal documents from the other side of the globe they do this to learn about an upcoming attack or gain knowledge of where the military is going or to steal plans of top-secret weapon governments are actively hacking into other governments this is the new norm governments have to take their cyber defense seriously if for nothing else than to protect their data from other governments but what is it really like when a government hacks into another government well that's the story you're about to read.

so let's ride shotgun along with our nation-state actor to hear exactly how they hack into another government this should be exciting so strap in and let's go for a ride first let's get the mission

The story starts here:

A couple of years ago we had a tasking to go after a network that belonged to a foreign government agency our task was to get access to it and gather specific information and the way the nation-state operations work is that the cyber elements of a nation-state don't derive requirements unto themselves they get it from someone else you know someone else in the government or an agency says we think this

information exists on that network to get access to the network but that's usually all the tasks is this task seems to only have a tiny amount of

information we've only given a foreign government agency's name some IP addresses and a general idea of what data to grab this is nowhere near enough

information to get started hacking into that network we don't know what tools to use or what computers to target once we're in we're gonna need more

information and the big thing for nation-states, in particular, we're not only the goal is, of course, to get access and collect your information but

overriding that goal is your need to state clandestine so not only do we gain more information but we need to get it secretly there are many reasons to stay

hidden when doing this mission first there could be political blowback another country could become furious if they caught us hacking into it another reason not to get caught is because of the equities of our tools exploits an infrastructure just like James Bond can't afford to lose this top-secret

spying technology a nation-state actor also uses cutting-edge hacking techniques that they don't want the target to be aware of these hacking

techniques can be very expensive and sometimes takes years of research and are worth millions of dollars so it's imperative that we stay as invisible as

possible while conducting this entire mission, oh and for this story let's pick a random country to use as an example target so let's go with the Peruvian

Ministry of Foreign Affairs the actual target will remain anonymous the military sometimes uses the term kill chain to describe how an attack takes place so the military calls this the preparation of the battlefield but the cyber sort of equivalent to that is the cyber kill chain this describes the

different phases of a cyber attack I'm going to explain what that means as we walk through this story there are seven phases to the cyber kill chain that must be conducted to complete an attack phase one is reconnaissance in this phase we need to gather information about the target like I said we have no idea what

type of exploit to use or what systems to attack so we begin by collecting information now I've got to figure out a way in so now it's things like passive reconnaissance and mapping so start figuring out what can we learn about this network without letting them know that we're trying to learn stuff about

it questions like how big is the network what kind of systems are on it hardware software what kind of antivirus is deployed there what is my access vector

so the team does a scan against a target power to see what is exposed to the Internet and they begin mapping what's visible to the world they have a website they're

hosting a web server that's within their environment so that's a box on the Internet with like Apache Tomcat running on it okay so that's good to know so now

I know that it's probably a Linux box and a web server that potentially has vulnerabilities I can exploit that's pretty interesting we find a couple of

things like that normally most governments and organizations keep their internet facing devices up-to-date this is important to do because an out-of-date system has a lot more security holes than one that's been updated but in this case, the web server was not fully patched which means the team can use a known vulnerability to access it and we start to come up with some potential avenues so now we have a potential point of entry into this

government's network that's still not enough information it's important to try to understand what exactly is in their network and it would be nice if we had a

map of where to go once we get in it would also be nice if we know who the people were at work in that office to get a sense of the team that's defending

that network and there are some tricky ways of figuring this out the way we can do that is that IT and if InfoSec people at large are pretty friendly open

and somewhat stupid often so let's go with the Peruvian Ministry of Foreign Affairs between Facebook and LinkedIn and whatever local Peruvian version of Facebook exists down there I can probably find somewhere between 50 to 100 to hundreds of people that work at that organization that have profiles on

those networks so I can start to collect full names and email addresses and maybe even position titles of people that work in there so I care about the IT

infrastructure the technical infrastructure so I'm looking for their IT people and their security people I bet I can find the systems administrator

or database administrator or someone that does like tea in that organization who has announced on the internet that they exist this is their

name and email address and this is what they do for that organization so once I start compiling all of that I'm gonna start looking for things that allow me

to tie them to the organization to the things they're using the best places to do that are I mean Google but more specifically Reddit is amazing for this

and then the technical forms that belong to products for example if I found on LinkedIn

or Facebook that Bob is an IT administrator at the Peruvian Ministry
of Foreign Affairs this gives me Bob's full name and email address I can then use Google to search his name and email address I find things like Bob's posting
on the Sigmund subreddit asking questions about why his Windows 2012 server is acting the way it is or him asking questions like I'm running a
Windows 2008 r2 box that's my domain controller do I need to update or not like do I don't really want to but what does everybody think should I do
that and when I find postings like that I can link them back to Bob I can confirm things like oh they're running a domain controller on Windows
2008 r2 box that's fantastic we find things in like antivirus and security forums since our target is to get specific data out of the network it's
likely that data exists in a database somewhere so the team looks through the people who worked there to try to find the database administrator or DBA I
found a DBA on Facebook or LinkedIn and he's a senior DBA he noted that he's an

expert on Oracle 11g cool so I can assume that they're probably running
Oracle roughly 11g inside their network and I have a team of people I have like 15 people who do nothing other than spent eight hours a day for six to eight
weeks searching scouring the Internet to collect the names email addresses and phone numbers of the people that work for my target organization
slim that number down to the ones that work there and the particular rules that I care about and then scour the internet for everything they publicly put out
there it has to do with anything technical and that gives us little tidbits about what we can expect to find in the environment after looking at the
data we've collected so far we have discovered an incredibly important piece of information I know the Oracle database that they have in their
environment likely has the data that I'm supposed to be collecting so after 15 people have worked full-time for two months gathering as much information as
they can on the target we now have a very detailed report we know who works there

what their roles are what kind of systems they run down to the version of software on those systems we now have a pretty good picture of their environment great so phase one is complete we now move on to Phase two of

the cyber kill chain weaponization I can now go to my leadership my management the ones who ostensibly owned the equities that I want to now use and I

can ask them for approval to do what I'm going to do equities are hacking techniques used to access a network or exploit some hacking techniques are

known to the public and are easier to get approval for because they cost nothing to acquire and if you're caught using the exploit it's hard to trace it

back to us since anyone in the world has access to that exploit but some exploits are expensive and top-secret these are harder to get approval for because if

you get caught the enemy could learn how to use your exploit but if you're caught using an exploit that nobody in the world knows about it narrows down who

could possibly have an exploit like that which could result in the attempted break-in to be traced back to us so I go to leadership and I say I have this tasking from these people to go after this network here's everything we know about the network these are the systems administrators these are the security people, these are the names email addresses and phone numbers based on data points ABCD and Ewe believe they're using this sort of antivirus and this sort of hardware we know they run you know web servers using Tomcat we know based on some other forum postings that they got Oracle database instances running on the inside so we put all that together and with those data points I derive the tools and exploits that I need to use knowing that before I get in I can get approval to use implant X with exploit Y that are specific to Oracle 11g so once I build out that case I can get approval and that approval is based on the risk posed to those equities given what I know about the environment so when I say I know that they are probably running this antivirus and these security tools I can say that I have these tools in these exploits and that I'm going to deploy in the network that is not detected by that antivirus

and the security system that they have I had now mitigated the biggest risk of getting caught rate which is a V or security systems flagging my tools or me

throwing exploits and if I can do that then I can get approvals to proceed and actually execute my operation so 60 days 90 days go by I built what's called a

targeting package and I've got operational approval to use the equities to complete the task so we now have a point of entry a map of the inside and

know whom to expect to be there when we arrive we also have all the specific exploits we need to execute this task this marks the end of our weaponize

Asian phase three of the cyber kill chain is delivery we need to actually send the exploit to the system in the network this is where the mission

begins to be dangerous from here on out any misstep could have terrible consequences because it could mean being caught if we were James Bond we'd now be fully geared up and ready for action so we figured out here is the internet-facing box

the web server that they're using was not patched wasn't
updated so I was able to actually use the known exploit to gain the right access to that machine once I did that I put an implant down on
that machine because it was pretty safe it was actually a Linux server and the nice thing about Linux is that you know no antivirus right so I'm not super
concerned and especially because it's a web server I don't worry about a user seeing the screen using it and see something weird going on but anyway so I
get down on that box sit there for a little bit everything looks pretty good I mean there's not much to see it's a web server and it's got a website on it
got a database back into it not a whole lot going on we are now in the foreign government's Network we have successfully infiltrated it's like we've snuck in
the building but we're only in the hallway using the data we've collected in the last few months we know we need to find the administrators computer to
gain control of it this leads us to the next phase of the cyber kill chain exploitation

because if we can get on the admin's computer chances are they
have all the keys to the kingdom and by using their machine we can access anything we want the nice thing about landing on a server like that is one thing that servers do have is admins logging in to them to administer them and that admin is going to log in and I'm probably going to be able to capture
his credentials or that admin is going to establish an authenticated session between that server and it hates the web server and the admin's machine and I'm
probably going to be able to float across that authenticated session and move laterally to the admin's machine there's a variety of ways that you can
do that but suffice to say it's either I'm capturing his credentials because he's going to log in to administer or I'm just gonna use his authenticated
session to move laterally over so the nice thing, in this case, was that we knew the admin you know like I said we had done a month of open source research
because we knew we were going to be exploiting the web server we knew who

their website administrator was we knew the team of people inside the network that responsible for maintaining the website the database that sat behind the website all the code associated with the website we knew all these people

developers are like the worst great like IT people post a lot of stuff on the internet security people post a little bit less stuff on the internet but

developers and web administrators and web admin they post everything on the Internet it's ridiculous so we found all of them and all their

content and we knew them all by name we had pictures of all the guys associated with a website we knew all these guys so what was great was that once we

exploited the web server we pretty much knew it was going to be one of three people that were going to log in and administer it so the plan was to simply

sit and wait for one of those three people to log in we thought we knew how they were going to log in because again we were familiar with the assistance they

had deployed we could tell by the configuration on the web server how we could expect to see them log into that machine so really it just became a waiting game for us sometimes waiting for an admin to log in can take a long time days weeks months one trick I've heard that hackers do is to sometimes cause a problem on the web server like make the CPU spike or crash an application but why do this well if the web server is acting problematic it will result in an admin logging in to troubleshoot it and when they do wow they've just walked into the trap but in our case, the waiting wasn't that long so one of the admin's logs in we see it happened we get the information that we need we move laterally onto his machine and we put the implant on his machine you just heard the fifth phase of the cyber kill chain installation we've just installed an implant on the target system an implant is a bug a Trojan a remote access tool it allows us to pretty much take ownership of that computer for those of you familiar with Metasploit just imagine basically something like

Metasploit on lots of steroids the next phase of the cyber kill chain is command and control just because the implant is on the Machine doesn't mean

it's going to do anything someone needs to tell it what to do and in this case, we now have the ability to remotely access the network admins computer this

is our command and control over the target computer we are now very close to finishing our mission all that's left is for us to take control of the admins

computer and then access the database and take the data we need so we wait a little while before getting into the admin's computer to not look suspicious

we waited about a day day and a half to go interactive on the box actually be using it interactively once we were using it interactively while the other person was using it we were logged on when they were which is generally the way that works we started looking at screenshots of the desktop and we saw a

browser open and we saw dozens of tabs open in the browser we started going through a lot of the screenshots and seeing the contents of the tabs and it

was the person googling this weird
behavior that Windows was doing the
administrator's computer that we have
infiltrated was acting strange
it was displaying lots of errors and certain
programs were crashing it definitely looked
like this admin had a virus of some kind
and at first we saw
that we're thinking well that's weird I
wonder if these problems on his computer
predate our presence there we didn't really
know but we had the sneaking suspicion
that had something to do with us so
unbeknownst to us and the time from when
we collected our information initially
through the open source and
when we put the implant down he had
upgraded his operating system he'd
upgraded Windows essentially to the next
version normally the worst case scenario
is that your implant doesn't work because
it's not compatible right for whatever
reason it's not compatible and just doesn't
work and that sucks and
you're really upset by that I would have
preferred that to be the outcome here
instead the implant worked from the extent
of it went down installed where

it should have and began operating as expected the problem was that it wasn't playing well with the newer version of Windows that was on that box and unfortunately started causing very odd Windows behavior and that very odd behavior took on like the worst possible version which was things that were very visible to the user so now that we're on the box and we know exactly what version of Windows it was we recreated it in our own lab environment so I know what the version of Windows it is and I know the hardware I basically rebuilt that same exact machine in our environment and tossed our implant on it and saw that our implant was causing this weird behavior so this is really really bad news for us because this is how you get caught great it was terrifying from the standpoint of

political blowback these things get like notifications of this sort of stuff goes up to the most senior levels of government right because when you get

caught on a network like this you have Prime Minister's calling each other so if things got bad enough we would have to be informed all the way up through the leadership of the agencies and all the way up into the senior leadership of government so everybody was very concerned at this point because we had already been on the web server we'd done a lot of work already we felt pretty comfortable so we were already deploying pretty sophisticated big implants onto

the network this one that was causing these problems was not a stage one loader this was a relatively sophisticated actually pretty sophisticated fully

featured implant at this point that we couldn't afford to lose nor could we afford to get caught on the network so once we realize what was happening you know

this is again the government rate so all the alarms start going off you have to start telling a lot of people have to start writing a lot of memos

and going to a lot of meetings to try to get everyone up to speed on what's happening what the risks are and what we're going to do any of

course now the first instinct is to delete it or removed in your implant unfortunately because it was already causing so many stability issues the concern was if we try to get to it to delete it, it might make it even worse we didn't know so the risk was don't do anything and right now he just thought

that he was having technical problems not that there was the security issue so we thought okay the risk is either stay with what we've got and written out the technical stuff and hope he doesn't figure out that it's not actually a technical problem it's a security problem or we try to delete it and cause

some other weird thing to happen that makes it even worse and then we're totally screwed so we decided to leave it and not delete it

and sort of take the bet and it got worse for about a week because not only do we watch them from googling for solutions to the problem like googling

the symptoms that he's seen in Windows we were reading his emails and seeing his chats with IT people telling them what was going on and putting in

trouble tickets and you know we saw the chat with his IT guy that was like hey can you come to my desk at like 2 o'clock to take a look and I mean we started you know that everyone started getting very concerned at that point more than we already were things are not going well at this point it's very tense

and concerning in the office the implant being used as an expensive secret if it was discovered it could result in tracing it back to the attackers and

losing this expensive and secret implant but at this point, we have successfully completed six out of the seven faces of the cyber kill chain there's only one phase left and that's doing the action on the objective in our case our objective is to use the administrator's

computer to get the data out of the Oracle database the team is hesitant about finishing the job well so the problem that it was a big Network and we knew the database that we wanted we knew that there was a database of a particular type that we want to get access to but we didn't know exactly

where it was on the network and at this the point we have a high risk of getting caught and the problem is you know we're watching them troubleshooting this and if they're troubleshooting and troubleshooting and troubleshooting and then at some point, they figure out that there's something real here and we need to call on the security people and start looking a little bit closer the last thing we would want to

would be to have a wider presence on the network even if it's on other machines elsewhere on the network that can at the moment that your incident response

gets involved and starts locking things down we're screwed so I fell point we want to minimize our presence to the least amount of exposure

that we can without losing our access so for now, that minimization was this computer that was on that's having the problem and the web server that was it

and be very very clear without even any debate decision was 60 quiet don't do anything let this play out because nobody wanted to increase the risk

profile until we knew how this was going to turn out to the team waits and watches days go by administrators trying to troubleshoot the errors they're seen

a week goes by he continues to troubleshoot and in the second week the admin asks for

help from IT yeah so the second week the
IT people are coming in
and they're looking at the computer and we
know that they're coming to the person's
desk because we see them setting up
appointments and we reached
this point where we can tell in the nature of
the trouble ticket that they've hit a dead
end they can't figure out why they can't
figure out what's
happening they can't figure out the reason
for what's happening you can't locate the
cause and it seems non-deterministic to
them you know why
it's happening I know what the implant is
doing and why it's causing Windows to
behave that way but since they don't know
the implants there to them the
behavior is entirely non-deterministic so
because it's non-deterministic they can't
devise the technical solution for it an
ultimate solution that they came
to was to just wipe it and start over it was a
fancy implant but it was just user level and
it was on the hard drive so at the moment
they wiped
the drive and reimaged it we were fine they
removed our implant and we were good it

was a significant relief thank God it's over but you know holy
are we all getting fired which is anyone's reasonable reaction to workplace events like that where things have gone wrong you're essentially in charge
of that group that where things went wrong it was all on me so there was that moment of you know I guess I'll get a box and pack up my desk
but eh it's the government so no one gets fired and that wasn't the outcome there's a whole post-mortem that we did after this to look at what
happened how it happened why it happened how to prevent it and you know the determination after the fact was there—
there was no negligence at play no one did anything wrong this is just what happened the chance of us doing two months of research taking 30 days to make decisions and have meetings and
then executing the operation in that thirty days one of the admins upgrading windows that's not a super high chance of that happening and we just got
unlucky right unfortunately like those two stars crossed in the sky and that happened

you know if it had been six months and we didn't try to re-update
her information and make it fresher then the outcome would likely have been he waited too long right you should have known that six months too much can change in
six months but 30 days was reasonable because I mean again the government it takes 30 days to push the paperwork and get meetings and just do the
administrative stuff you need to do so the fact that that happened in 30 days that guy updated the windows box that was seen as acceptable the only other
the fallout was when we moved laterally onto that machine you know should we have done anything tactically before we put the implant down on that box
and there was this debate on that should we have captured the credentials and just interactively and interacted with that machine just to capture things
like its OS and antivirus and all that that was an operational decision that we made at the time a very tactical decision but because we had done the

open source and we knew what was there–
there were seemingly less cause to do it and
that was it so with the implant cleaned off
the machine, the team can
relax knowing their cover isn't going to be
blown and they're expensive exploit won't
be discovered what about that initial
objective to get access to the
the database we never got access to the
database not because of this and just ended
up being that the network was configured
in such a way
that our path to get there was extremely
complicated from where we were on the
network to where we needed to get to and
like any other business environment we
had competing requirements so you know
at some point probably I don't know a
month and a half after this incident after
this small incident you know we
came to this point where okay I know
where the Oracle server is I know who the
admins are but our ability to get to it as
complicated is going to take a
a little while we can do it but do we want to
do it and at the same time I had three other
requirements that I had to satisfy and those
requirements required

some of the same people that I was
currently using to work on this one so it
was sort of like what do we do do we just
you know cut bait and walk away or
do we just all in and go for it we decided to
cut bait and walk away and that happens all
the time just because I think any hacker
whether
you're a nation-state a BT or you know
your kid in your mom's basement everyone
knows that it's a lot of luck that stuff works
only so much thought and
intelligence goes into it it's a lot of luck at
the end of the day and I'd say statistically
in my years doing it the luck isn't there or
runs out more than
half of the amount of time just because it's
hard right and getting harder because
people are just in general more aware of
cybersecurity and information
security and they're slightly smarter just
enough to know maybe not to click on a
link or maybe not to visit that website from
work or your computer
and maybe don't click okay when it says
flash needs to update so there are just
enough people that are just enough smarter
where this is getting just that much

harder every single day.

The story ends here, thanks for reading the whole book.